THE GOLDEN RING

SERGIEV POSAD · PEREYASLAVL-ZALESSKY · ROSTOV THE GREAT · UGLICH
YAROSLAVL · KOSTROMA · VLADIMIR · BOGOLIUBOVO
SUZDAL · YURYEV-POLSKOY

I V A N   F I O D O R O V   A R T   P U B L I S H E R S

The "Golden Ring" is a tourist route running through a series of cities and towns in central Russia, which are remarkable for their ancient history and abundance of historical and cultural monuments. The area they occupy became the centre of Russia in the twelfth century, after Kiev, "the mother of Russian cities", had lost its leading role in political and cultural life. The steadily growing pressure of the nomads from the southern steppes resulted in a large-scale migration of the population to the northeast, to the lands of the Vladimir-Suzdal Principality, where dense woods provided protection from the steppe cavalry. Peasants, warriors, craftsmen, icon-painters and monks had to leave the familiar surroundings and move to the new places by rare roads or by waterways carrying with themselves a memory of the past glories of their homeland. This accounts for the names of rivers and towns in these lands, which were characteristic of the south Russian dialects, sometimes specifying the locality – for example, Pereyaslavl-Zalessky (meaning Pereyaslavl-Beyond-the-Woods).

Natural environment was of major significance in the emergence and flowering of the present-day "Golden Ring" area, which strikes even the present-day traveller's imagination by a variety of its landscapes. Since time immemorial it has attracted people by the abundance of waterways, vast fields devoid of forests and having a fertile soil, large resources of building timber and deposits of so-called "white stone" – the beautiful architectural material called the "marble of ancient Russia".

The cities of the "Golden Ring" grew to become the capitals of the principalities where religious life and arts were thriving. They were also important points on the trade routes between the North and the South, Europe and Asia. Many churches and fortified structures, dwelling houses and trade buildings have survived to this day in the area. Museum collections preserve true masterpieces of icon-painting and applied arts, and the interiors of churches are decorated with magnificent frescoes. A visit to these places will enable tourists to form a fairly good idea of the specific mode of life and culture of ancient and present-day Russia.

SERGIEV POSAD

Sergiev Posad does not rank among the oldest towns of the "Golden Ring", but it occupies an exceptionally prominent place in Russian culture and history. The very name of the town, meaning 'Sergius's Settlement', has a profound sense – it is associated with Russia's most brilliant spiritual leader St Sergius of Radonezh, the saint of the Orthodox Church revered in Russia for many centuries. St Sergius founded in this area a secluded monastic abode. Soon the *skete* grew into a monastery and a settlement developed around it. The settlement gathered all sorts of people related to the life of the monastery, especially craftsmen, who laid the beginnings of some famous artistic handicrafts flourishing at Sergiev Posad and around it to this day. One of tourist attractions here is the market remarkable for a wide choice of souvenirs made by local craftsmen, especially pieces of woodwork decorated in a variety of techniques.

The picturesque complex of buildings of the Trinity–St Sergius Monastery or *Laura* (*laura* is one of a few Russia's most important monasteries to which even the Tsars thought it honourable to make a pilgrimage on foot), which has organically blended with the lovely surrounding scenery, has been shaped in the course of several centuries. The earliest of its structures date back to the early Middle Ages, while one of the latest, the bell-tower,

THE GOLDEN RING

to the eighteenth century. The vertical of the Baroque bell-tower thrusting upwards does not clash with the whole. Moreover, it even looks like a powerful chord in the architectural ensemble of the monastery which is distinguished by a striking compositional unity despite all the stylistic difference of its buildings. The panorama of the monastery is perceived like a symbol of Russian culture, so heterogeneous and yet integral.

The role of the monastery is associated not only with spiritual and religious problems but with general historical events, too. The monastery is skirted by the defensive walls, which were erected in the sixteenth and seventeenth centuries and proved their might several times. First of all, at the beginning of the seventeenth century, during the Time of Trouble, the Trinity–St Sergius Monastery withstood a siege by the army of the Polish-Lithuanian invaders. At the end of the seventeenth century the young Peter I took shelter within the walls of the *laura* twice. He hid there, together with his sister Sophia and brother Ivan, during the uprising of the Streltsy in 1682. And in 1688, when the young co-tsars' elder sister Sophia, the Regent, seized the control of the state, Peter again had to flee to the Trinity–St Sergius Monastery. The eleven towers of the fortress walls acquired their present-day appearance in the seventeenth and eighteenth centuries, which predetermined their larger decorativeness, in comparison with the austere functionality of the earlier structures. This quality is particularly noticeable in the design and decoration of the corner tower, known as the

Corn (or Duck) Tower from which Peter the Great, as tradition has it, liked to shoot ducks coming to the nearby pond.

The unquestionable authority of the founder of the monastery provided from the fourteenth century onwards an influx of the best intellectual and artistic forces, a flood of rich donations from noted statesmen and the richest families. The settlements of Sergiev Posad had many workshops of craftsmen who excelled in making crosses, ladles, silversmiths and other artistic objects. Thanks to all these factors the Treasury of the Trinity–St Sergius Monastery and the State Museum of History and Art in Sergiev Posad possess unique collections of veritable treasures. Of especial interest among them are works by jewellers skilled in various techniques and pieces of embroidery. These masterpieces of "painting in needlework" are executed so skilfully that, as evidenced by Paolo of Aleppo who visited Russia in the seventeenth century, they could be taken for painted works. From the first years

←

1. Panoramic view of the Trinity–St Sergius Laura (Monastery)

2. Trinity–St Sergius Monastery. Red or Fine Gate.
16th–19th century. Central entrance to the laura

3. Shroud depicting St Sergius of Radonezh. Ca 1424.
Museum of History and Art, Sergiev Posad

4. Cross. 17th century. By master craftsman Andrei Malov.
Museum of History and Art, Sergiev Posad

of its existence the monastery was the cultural centre where manuscript books were copied and talented writers worked, the most famous of which were Epiphany the Wise and Maxim the Greek.

There are many first-rate architectural monuments at Sergiev Posad outside the *laura*, such as the Chapel of St Paraskeva-over-the-Well – a unique structure of the turn of the seventeenth and eighteenth centuries. It embodies the most typical features of the "Moscow Baroque": the plastic expressiveness of elaborate details and clear-cut articulation of volumes. The chapel standing on the low land, at the foot of the hill dominated by the monastery, seems to meet travellers arriving from Moscow.

And still the most interesting buildings determining the image of Sergiev Posad can be found in its heart, the *laura*. The principal feature of the monastery ensemble is the bell-tower, which dominates the town as a whole and is visible even from beyond the town's borders. Its silhouette soaring to the height of more

5. *Chapel of St Paraskeva-over-the-Well.*
Late 17th – early 18th century

6. *Religious procession in the Trinity–St Sergius Monastery*

7. *Trinity–St Sergius Monastery. Bell-tower. 1740–70. Architects Johann Jacob Schumacher, Ivan Michurin and Dmitry Ukhtomsky*

than eighty metres produces an impression of lightness unusual for a structure of the eighteenth-century advanced Baroque. This effect is accomplished by a special device – the preservation of the width of spans on all the tiers reducing upwards.

The monastery was built in the course of several centuries. In the age of St Sergius the monastery was wooden and according to the available data, only the first Cathedral of the Holy Trinity that has not come down to us was built in stone. The largest structure of the complex is the Cathedral of the Assumption (1559–85) dedicated to the Mother of God especially revered in Russia. The building repeats in its basic proportions and constructions the Cathedral of the Assumption in the Moscow Kremlin that was the central cathedral of the Orthodox Church and was based, in turn, on the forms of the most ancient and highly prized Cathedral of the Assumption in Vladimir. The exterior of the cathedral attracts one's attention by the stately appearance of its modestly adorned façades articulated by pilaster-strips. In the middle of the eighteenth century the domes acquired bulbous shapes and the drum of the central, predominant dome was raised over the others and wholly covered with gilding while the four corner ones were decorated with gilt stars on a dark blue background. The murals in the interior, recalling the Yaroslavl wall paintings in their style, and the tall many-tiered iconostasis date from the late seventeenth century. By the northwestern corner of the cathedral is situated the not very conspicuous burial vault of the Godunov family. By orders of the Pretender the body of Boris Godunov was taken out of the burial vault in the Cathedral of the Archangel Michael in the Kremlin and after being kept for some time in a Moscow monastery was transferred to the Trinity–St Sergius Monastery that was patronized and generously donated by Boris Godunov.

In the second half of the nineteenth century, the merchant Riumin gave money for the construction, next to the Cathedral of the Assumption, of a canopied fountain pool. The shape of this structure is stylized in keeping with the notions of that time about the character of old Russian art

Of great interest is the Chapel of St Paraskeva-over-the-Well (late 17th century). The large and richly adorned building with many elaborate details happily contrasts with the monumental shapes of the cathedrals and bell-tower. The elaborate silhouette is typical of the "Moscow (or Naryshkin) Baroque", notably of the so-called tiered churches. The rectangular base supports three consequently surmounted octagonal tiers, which creates a complex dynamic effect of the masses. The polychrome decor of the façade and the use of materials different in texture further enhance the picturesque impression.

Simultaneously with the erection of the fountain pool the interior of the gateway Church of St John the Baptist was redesigned. As a result an eclectic complex has been shaped, which combines the architectural elements of the late seventeenth century (when the church was built) and decorative wall

8. Trinity–St Sergius Monastery.
The Cathedral of the Assumption (1559–85), the Chapel of St Paraskeva-over-the-Well (late 17th century), the burial vault of the Godunov family (1780) and the fountain pool (1872)

9. Trinity–St Sergius Monastery. Cathedral of the Assumption. Interior

10. Trinity–St Sergius Monastery.
Gateway Church of St John the Baptist. 1699

SERGIEV POSAD

THE GOLDEN RING

painting in the spirit of the nineteenth century, with the icons executed in an academic manner and the gorgeous, richly decorated Empire-style iconostasis.

The Cathedral of the Holy Trinity (1422), much smaller than the Cathedral of the Assumption, is the spiritual and historical centre of the *laura*. The cathedral put up during the time of St Sergius suffered in 1408, during a fire in the monastery, a great damage. The monastery was burnt down by the Mongol-Tartar invaders who took vengeance on it for the edification and blessing by St Sergius of Prince Dmitry Donskoy and the Russian warriors for the historic Battle of Kulikovo. The present-day cathedral, built by St Sergius's successor, Hegumen Nikon, became the place where the holy relics of St Sergius are kept. It is also the place firmly associated in believers' notions with another Russian saint, the great artist Andrei Rublev. Fully aware how complex and important the task was, Nikon literally implored Rublev and his friend Daniel Chorny to start painting frescoes of the cathedral. The fact that such outstanding masters were responsible for the painted decor of the interiors and that the world-famous icon *The Trinity* was painted for this iconostasis determined an exclusive role of the cathedral in national culture. The exterior of this architectural monument is also marked by aesthetic perfection. Built along the lines of Moscow architecture, this relatively small and moderately adorned cathedral attracts great attention. It harmoniously combines the emphasis on stability and steadiness by a slight inclination of the walls inwards with a lightness and elegance, which is enhanced by the height of the graceful drum and the pointed keel-shaped elements completing the semicircular arched gables and the portal.

The idea of unity and integrity embodied in the abstract form of the proportions and structures of the cathedral, is perfectly realized by means of painting in *The Trinity* by Andrei Rublev. This endows the Cathedral of the Holy Trinity, where the silver shrine containing the relics of St Sergius of Radonezh is kept, with a special significance of the earliest memorial church building in Russia. The shrine, an outstanding work of decorative art in its own right, was produced in 1585 by orders of Ivan the Terrible. In the eighteenth century a Baroque canopy was set over the shrine and a railing was erected around it. A never ending line of pilgrims attracted to this holy place by a common desire to bow to the remains which are holy for each Russian, vividly illustrates the vital character of the idea of unity formulated by the saint. Despite the invariable presence of numerous believers, the interior of the cathedral evokes a state of concentration. One is overwhelmed by the expectation of a miracle at the tomb of the saint. The interior owes much of this special atmosphere to the thoroughly calculated system of lighting. The windows, with all their large dimensions are located so that they are practically unnoticed and do not let much light in. The resulting semidarkness corresponds to the edifying words of St Cyril of Belozerye, one of the pillars of the Orthodox Church: "...stand in the church with fear and trepidation." The Chapel of St Nikon

11. Trinity–St Sergius Monastery. Cathedral of the Holy Trinity (1422). Chapel of St Nikon (1548)

12. Festive day in the Trinity–St Sergius Monastery

13. Trinity–St Sergius Monastery. Cathedral of the Holy Trinity. Iconostasis and the shrine with the relics of St Sergius of Radonezh

was attached to the cathedral more than a hundred years after its construction. It developed on a smaller scale and in lighter proportions the plastic idea of the Cathedral of the Holy Trinity. The chapel preserves the shrine with the holy relics of the second hegumen of the monastery, St Nikon.

The Church of the Holy Spirit (1476) plays a special role in the composition of the square – standing in front of the cathedral it links the earlier structures with their austere and concise features and bright-coloured decorative structures of the seventeenth and eighteenth centuries. Built at the end of the fifteenth century and modelled on the churches designed for the installation of bells over them, the Church of the Holy Spirit has elongated proportions in its upper tier for functional purposes. The basic volume was correspondingly made more slender and the profiles of the *zakomaras* or semicircular arched

14. *Trinity–St Sergius Monastery. Church of the Holy Spirit. 1476*

15. *Trinity–St Sergius Monastery. Royal Chambers. Late 17th century*

16. *Domes of the Church of the Holy Spirit and the Church of St Micah*

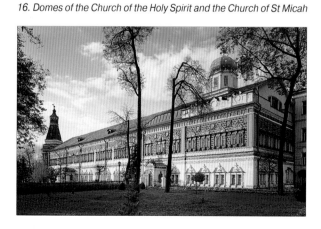

THE GOLDEN RING

gables and *kokoshniks*, their purely decorative counterparts, as well as the clustered semi-columns on pilaster-strips were made more refined. The juxtaposition of the two churches vividly demonstrates the evolution of Russian ecclesiastical architecture in the fifteenth century and marks two opposite trends in it. The Cathedral of the Holy Trinity looks like a Russian epic hero while the Church of the Holy Spirit appears as the beautiful Russian maiden.

The magnificent *Trinity* by Andrei Rublev is acknowledged to be both a masterpiece of world art and an object of religious adoration retaining its role throughout centuries. Its example vividly illustrates the essence of the Orthodox faith admitting the double essence of the world. In such concept equally significant is both physical and spiritual perfection. So Russian icon-painting demonstrates in its supreme accomplishments the visible harmony of lines and colours suggested by the real life itself without discarding, however, the conventional character of depiction. Thus it did not repeat the way of European painting, which sought to attain during the Renaissance the utmost verisimilitude of visual observations. On the contrary, the rendering of the symbolic meaning and of the most abstract general notions during the Russian Renaissance, connected primarily with the work of the great Andrei Rublev, became the essential task of Russian icon-painting. Indeed, many people see in *The Trinity* primarily the visual representation of theological notions on the harmony of cosmogonic principles. The three figures are inscribed in an imaginary circle as a symbol of absolute balance. The hand of the central angel blessing the bowl indicates its centre. But this is not just a bowl from the table laid hurriedly by the elderly hospitable owners and their servants to treat wayfarers – as artists before Rublev used to interpret this subject. This is the symbolic bowl of Christ's redemptive sacrifice and His suffering for the entire mankind, the bowl of the New Testament. The silhouette of the bowl occurs several times in the icon – in the space

between the angels' figures and in the outlines of their stretched wings. This is to emphasize the Christian message of the composition, and many researchers treat the images of the icon as the New Testament Trinity: God the Father, Christ and the Holy Spirit. But no less right are those who appreciate to the human vein in Rublev's work, the beauty and variety of emotional shades in the countenances and gestures of the angels, and the similarity of the icon's chromatic range with the colours of that pleasant time in Russia when crops and other earthly fruits are ripening under the bright blue sky.

The Trinity has always been an especially revered iconic image. Icon-painters produced several variations of Rublev's impeccable composition and the icon itself acquired a superb golden mount thanks to the three Tsars, Ivan the Terrible, Boris Godunov and Mikhail Romanov. This priceless work, manufactured with the use of a number of complicated jewellery processes, is an illustrious example of the supreme level of craftsmanship in Russia and the superb virtuosity of its makers. It might be interesting to mention that there were two similar images of *The Trinity* in the local tier of the iconostasis: Boris Godunov commissioned a copy of the icon and a brilliant mount for it.

Before the nineteenth century the historical and purely artistic value of the icon as a unique work of art was underestimated. It was only at the beginning of the twentieth century, after the mount of *The Trinity* by Andrei Rublev was removed and a scrupulous cleaning of the image from the accretions

17. Andrei Rublev. The Trinity. *Early 15th century. Tretyakov Gallery, Moscow*

18. Mount of the icon of The Trinity *by Andrei Rublev.*
Late 16th – mid-17th century. Museum of History and Art, Sergiev Posad

19. Trinity–St Sergius Monastery.
Gateway Church of St John the Baptist. 1699

20. *Shroud:* The Appearance of the Mother of God to St Sergius of Radonezh. *1525. Museum of History and Art, Sergiev Posad*

21. *Phelonion. 1640–80. Museum of History and Art, Sergiev Posad*

22. *Mitre. Early 17th century. Museum of History and Art, Sergiev Posad*

THE GOLDEN RING

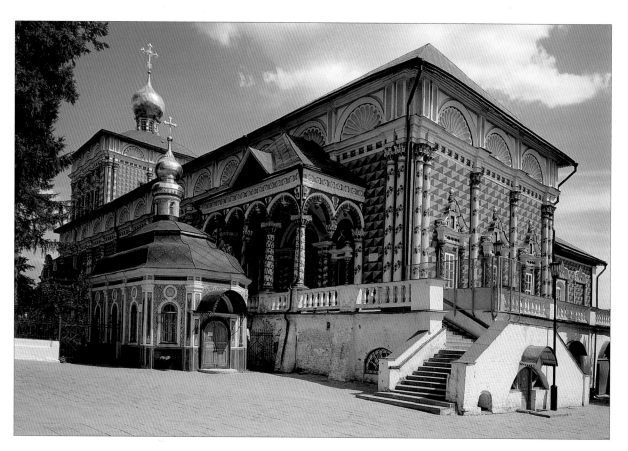

of grime and later overpaintings was carried out, that people could see the true mastery of the great icon-painter. The effect of the cleaned icon caused the shock of wonder among painters, historians of art and art-lovers.

The turn of the seventeenth and eighteenth centuries marked the end of the Middle Ages in Russian culture. The sunset of traditional art was especially vivid and artistic forms attained an especial decorative quality. A number of buildings were constructed during this period at the monastery in the "Moscow Baroque" style. These include the gateway Church of St John the Baptist erected near the Red Gate, the main entrance to the *laura*, built with the use of funds of the "noted guests", or the Stroganov merchants, the Tsar's Chambers as well as the Refectory with the Church of St Sergius rich in expressive plastic, colouristic and ornamental details. A striving towards ultimate "enlivening" of the plane characteristic of the

European Baroque did not prevent Russian architects to retain the clarity and integrity of volumes. This quality can be seen in the abundance and unusual complexity of various elements of window surrounds (platbands, twisted columns, balusters, etc.), in the polychrome painting of the walls with a "diamond" rustication imitating the masonry of hewn coloured blocks and in the use of materials differing in texture, notably glazed majolica tiles. As a result the buildings began to look like fairy-tale palaces made of precious materials.

23. Trinity–St Sergius Monastery. Refectory. Detail of the façade

24. Trinity–St Sergius Monastery. Refectory with the Church of St Sergius (1686–92); the Church of St Micah (1734)

→

25. Trinity–St Sergius Monastery. Interior of the Refectory

PEREYASLAVL-ZALESSKY

Leaving behind the bright-coloured Trinity–St Sergius Monastery, travellers continue their way northwards along the picturesque highway. Descents alternate here with upgrade slopes that afford fine perspective views of the surrounding grounds. Soon a magnificent view of Pereyaslavl-Zalessky, a town located on the shores of Lake Pleshcheyevo, one of the largest and most beautiful in Central Russia, appears in the distance.

The environs of Pereyaslavl-Zalessky, convenient for habitation, agricultural pursuits and fishing have been inhabited from time immemorial, as evidenced by the remains of ancient settlements and barrows as well as by the Kleshchino site of a later date and the legendary "Blue Stone", a pagan deity. This huge boulder brought here from Scandinavia in the ice age made mysterious migrations about the lakeshore during the recent centuries, rose from the bottom of the lake and from a pit in which it was buried on the order of church authorities.

The city, founded by the energetic Prince Yury Dolgoruky in 1152, derived its name from the other, earlier Pereyaslav located to the south-east of Kiev, at the place where the Trubezh River flows into the Dnieper. The river running through Pereyaslavl also bears the name of Trubezh. Such borrowing of place-names was the prince's thought-out step – he wanted to attract settlers from the south and at the same time to emphasize the continuity of his power from the princes of the glorious times of Kievan Russia. Pereyaslavl the New, as it was then called, was encircled by earthen ramparts, which survived thanks to the several layers of oak logs embedded in them. The high ramparts with fortress walls, the rivers Trubezh and its tributary Murmazh as well as a swampy lowland around, all that turned the town into an impregnable citadel.

Between 1238 and 1253 the ruler of Pereyaslavl was Prince Alexander Nevsky, who became famous due to his victories over the knights of the Livonian order. In February 1238 the town was

sacked and devastated by the Tartar-Mongol hordes. The prince restored urban structures, walls and towers destroyed and burnt down by the enemy.

In the course of subsequent centuries Pereyaslavl stretched for several miles along the shore of the lake occupying the space between the two hills flanking the valley near the lake. On the northern hill at the end of the eleventh century the Monastery of St Nicetas, the oldest in the area behind the Volga, was founded (the surviving stone structures date from the 16th to the 19th century). The monastery derives its name from that of the local saint Nicetas the Stylite, a repentant usurer, tax collector in Pereyaslavl. Next to the monastery is the Nicetas spring popular for its curative water.

In the second half of the eighteenth century Pereyaslavl markedly grew to become a significant trade centre. The St Alexander Nevsky Church of the Presentation in the Temple (1776) stands out among the numerous churches of this period, basically Baroque in design. The appearance of this church, especially the columned porticoes added later, betray the influence of the new, more lucid and concise style – Classicism.

The northern elevation affords a panoramic view of the town with the Goritsky Monastery of the Assumption in the south. The Goritsky Monastery was founded in the fourteenth century in the reign of Ivan Kalita at the southern approaches to the town, near the road from Moscow and Sergiev Posad. The strategic position of the monastery made it especially vulnerable to enemy's attacks and it was repeatedly assaulted and burnt down. Only structures dating from the seventeenth to nineteenth century have reached us. Of greatest interest in terms of architecture is the eastern corner within the monastery fence where the palace of the guard and the two gates adjoining it are situated – the Saint Gate in the south, with the gateway Church of St Nicholas, and the Passage Gate in the east. The Passage Gate is an example of the decorative trend characteristic of local architecture. It is revealed in the sumptuous and varied decor of figured bricks. An exclusion were only moulded ridge-pieces, naive but not devoid of a charm. The pediment of the rocaille type was erected later. The Passage Gate looks especially ornate on a sunny day in an intense light, when interlacing light and shade patterns play on the high relief of the masonry work.

←
26. Goritsky Monastery of the Assumption. 17th–18th century

27. Panoramic view of Pereyaslavl-Zalessky. On the left, the Church of the Presentation in the Temple (1776)

28. Goritsky Monastery of the Assumption. The Passage Gate. 17th century

29. Goritsky Monastery of the Assumption. Church of All Saints and the Refectory. 17th–18th century

Nowadays the monastery houses the Museum of History and Art that owns one of the best and diverse collections in Russian provincial towns. Deserving special attention is the department of woodwork including carved icons and pieces of sculpture. Among the most prized exhibits in the collection of painting are canvases by Ivan Shishkin, Konstantin Makovsky, Henryk Siemiradzki, Alexander Benois and Zinaida Serebriakova. The museum also preserves an assemblage of works by the well-known Soviet artist and teacher Dmitry Kardovsky, who bequeathed his mansion to the Union of Artists for organizing a centre for creative work.

The two wooden chapels brought to the monastery for a display from the villages of Pereyaslavl District emphasize the grandeur of the Cathedral of the Assumption. The cathedral has several distinctive features of the Baroque style: the elaborate plan, many-tiered design, figure-shaped window surrounds, diverse pilasters articulating the walls and the drums of the domes. The inner decor amazes one by an exceedingly lavish decoration. The walls and vaults are adorned with murals as well as with numerous moulded decorations, ornamental panels and representations of cherubs and angels. The elegant white stuccowork effectively contrasts with the light blue tinting of the flat parts of the walls. A special mention

30. View of the Goritsky Monastery of the Assumption

31. Goritsky Monastery of the Assumption.
Cathedral of the Assumption. Mid-18th century

32. Goritsky Monastery of the Assumption.
Cathedral of the Assumption. Interior

THE GOLDEN RING

should be made of the carved and gilt many-tiered iconostasis. This work of art was produced by the Russian craftsman Yakov Zhukov and includes architectural details of an elaborate profile, sculptural groups and various ornamental motifs.

Not far from the fortress rampart is the Monastery of St Nicholas where reconstruction work is under way now. The surviving sections of the walls and small turrets show the evolution of monastery railings from fortified structures to decorative ones. The Monastery of St Daniel, remarkable for the expressive silhouette of its architectural ensemble, is another major architectural landmark in the area of the Church of the Presentation in the Temple and the Goritsky Monastery. It preserves the murals painted

33. Monastery of St Nicholas. These domes will soon decorate the Cathedral of St Nicholas (late 17th century, restored in 1993)

34. Convent of St Theodore. Church of the Presentation in the Temple. 1710

35. In the environs of Pereyaslavl-Zalessky

by a team led by the well known Kostroma artist Gury Nikitin. Further southwards stands the Convent of St Theodore, with its oldest buildings dated from the distant age of Ivan the Terrible.

Pereyaslavl-Zalessky attracts artists from entire Russia by the variety of its architectural landmarks and its picturesque surroundings. The focus of Red Square in Pereyaslavl is the Cathedral of the Transfiguration, which is of the same age as the town itself. Resolved in austere and concise forms, it is markedly different from the richly adorned cathedrals of Vladimir dating from the same period. It has also very little in common with the diverse local churches built in the eighteenth century. The latter often have polychrome façades and are elaborate in plan in keeping with the Baroque style. A typical example is the Church of St Simeon standing on the road to Rostov. The local churches also often show, as for instance the Church of the Forty Martyrs, the ingenuity of their elaborate decorative details similar to those of window surrounds.

The Church of the Forty Martyrs stands at the spot where the Trubezh flows into Lake Pleshcheyevo and for more than two centuries serves as a guiding landmark to the residents of the Fishing Settlement stretching over the banks of the slow, picturesque Trubezh. The river and especially the lake have shaped the specific features of Pereyaslavl. It was on this lake that Peter the Great began to build his toy fleet, which marked the burgeoning of Russia's maritime power. The only surviving ship from that flotilla is *Fortune* housed in a special building put up for its preservation.

36. Cathedral of the Transfiguration. 1152–57

37. Church of St Simeon the Stylite. 1771

38. Church of the Forty Martyrs (of the Forty Saints). 1775

39. On the Trubezh River

ROSTOV THE GREAT

Rostov is one of the oldest Russian towns. Favourable natural conditions attracted people to this area from time immemorial. Archaeologists found here a large site of the Ugro-Finnish tribe Merya, which is reflected in the common name of the region – "the Chud's end" (the Chud is an Ugro-Finnish people). *The Russian Primary Chronicle* contains evidence that Rostov existed even in the pre-Christian era. The new religion met with a stubborn opposition of pagan priests – the magi. One of the preachers of the new faith, Leonty, was killed in 1071, but his friend Avraamy still succeeded in founding a monastery in this place. The town formed around the monastery quickly grew to be called "the Great" in the twelfth century, like Novgorod. This was promoted by close political contacts, with Byzantium in particular, as well as by an intense trade and cultural exchange. At the beginning of the thirteenth century Rostov became the seat of the grand duke and such well-known centres as Vladimir, Tver, Yaroslavl, Uglich and even Moscow were then subordinate to it. Further on, however, Rostov lost its political significance, although it retained its role as a very important religious, educational and cultural centre. The immense library of the monastery attracted to Rostov many theologians and men of letters who made a large contribution to Russian culture. One should mention primarily St Epiphany the Wise, the author of

the *Life of St Sergius of Radonezh*, and St Stephan of Perm, who created an alphabet for the Zyrians (the Zyrian or Komi language belongs to the Ugro-Finnish group). There were eminent women in Rostov too. Princess Maria, the widow of the hero Prince Vasilk, who was martyred in the Tartar imprisonment in the thirteenth century, entered the annals as a unique woman-chronicler. There were also warriors among Rostov women, who put on men's clothes and, sword in hand, fought their enemies.

The dramatic history of the town – internecine feuds of the principalities, the nomads' incursions and the devastating Polish-Lithuanian-Swedish intervention of the early seventeenth century – gave to early historical monuments little chance for survival. But it was in the seventeenth century too that Rostov quickly flourished. This happened in the 1630s when life resumed its natural course little by little. Instead of the medieval town, practically erased by the invaders in 1608, a new ensemble, rather compact in area and with a small number of buildings, but strikingly integral and harmonious, stretched in a picturesque way alongside Lake Nero. The complex of the Rostov Kremlin has long ago deservedly became a Mecca for tourists. Even at a distance, coming from Pereyaslavl-Zalessky in the south, you will hardly overlook the lake spreading amidst the plain and the fanciful silhouette emerging behind it and evoking, as it were, a certain musical rhythm.

The unique Rostov ensemble owes much of its unity to the will and taste of one man, who was destined to supervise the creation of this architectural masterpiece. Rostov gained its present-day appearance between 1660 and 1690, under Metropolitan Jonah. An outstanding ecclesiastical figure, one of the most educated men of his time, he passed a test and temptation of the highest power becoming the Patriarch or rather fulfilling the patriarchal duties during the period of Patriarch Nikon's disfavour. It is difficult to say what made Jonah cede the position back to Nikon who suddenly returned from his exile, despite the Tsar's decision. Probably Nikon's rare willpower and temperament played an important role in this event. It is likely that Jonah preferred the almost unlimited power in his eparchy to the life in the capital full of intrigues and a necessity to subordinate to the Tsar. The ensemble created under Jonah's supervision is in fact the metropolitan's court rather than a kremlin or citadel – the presence of mighty walls with battlements should not mislead us. The fortress-like character of the complex is a tribute to the tradition of building monasteries as fortified structures and Jonah's desire to make his residence similar to the Moscow Kremlin and to the main ecclesiastical centres such as the Trinity–St Sergius *Laura* or the New Jerusalem Monastery. As for practical defensive purposes, a system of walls was constructed on the ramparts, the remains of which are still visible in the town. A desire to attain the utmost outward effect of the ensemble is reflected in a whole number of absolutely original solutions in the design and decor of the buildings and certainly in the emergence of a distinct Rostov type of churches and fortress towers. The functional properties were partly realized in the towers: they had special places for watchmen, but the elaborate Baroque outlines of the tent-shaped tops certainly did not enhance the impression of stability and firmness.

←
40. Domes of the Rostov Kremlin

41. The Kremlin. Gateway Church of St John the Divine. 1683

42. The Kremlin. Gateway Church of St John the Divine. Interior

43. The Kremlin. Gateway Church of St John the Divine.
Galleries and portal

The churches of the Rostov Kremlin are tall, slender and as a rule two-tiered. Usually these are gateway churches on *podklet* or undercroft. As concerns the Church of St John the Divine, this building is flanked by two towers which indicate the entrance to the Kremlin on the side of the town. The same compositional motif is used in the Church of the Resurrection. Its overall vertical thrust is enhanced by the close arrangement of the drums, their energetic proportions and the pointed tops of the *zakomaras* or semicircular arched gables. The overall system of the Kremlin complex is unique – its buildings were linked by a network of concealed passages allowing one to walk around all the buildings of the Metropolitan's court without descending to the ground.

An orientation of Metropolitan Jonah, the builder of the Rostov Kremlin, towards Moscow also served as a reason for the construction of the Assembly Belfry (1682–87) and for casting unique

44, 47. Gateway Church of St John the Divine

45. The Kremlin. Red or Fine Chambers. 1670–80

46. The large bell of the Kremlin belfry

THE GOLDEN RING

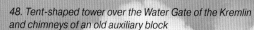

48. Tent-shaped tower over the Water Gate of the Kremlin and chimneys of an old auxiliary block

49. View of the walls and towers of the Kremlin from the Kremlin belfry

50. The Kremlin. Tower over the Water Gate. Late 17th century

bells for it. The Rostov bell chimes won general renown as the most expressive in Russia. Almost all the bells in the Kremlin have their own names. The largest bell, "Sysoi", weighs 2,000 *pouds* (about 600 lb.). Nowadays an idea of the Rostov complex of chimes, this largest musical instrument of the seventeenth century, can be gained only from tuning-forks in the local museum exactly reproducing the ringing of the ancient bells.

     The Rostov Kremlin became one of the last masterpieces of Russian medieval art and culture. The architecture of "Jonah's" buildings is not as sumptuous as that of structures of the "Moscow Baroque", but even smaller details of this ensemble are very beautiful. Thus, architects transformed into real works of art even functional structures such as chimneys. Two essential principles of medieval art are employed in their design. The first is the effective use of the rhythm created by the limited number of decorative details, in this case by fasciae, cornices and arches, for attaining a greater expression. The second one is a varied repetition of the three-dimensional motif: the chimneys of the old auxiliary block are somewhat different from one another in their shapes and proportions. At the same time each of them is slightly reminiscent of the hipped-roof tower over the Water Gate. The forms of the tower itself demonstrate one more principle, that of free symmetry. The volumes of the tower are visually perceived

THE GOLDEN RING

as stable and symmetric, but the arch of the gate shifted from the centre and the richly decorated annex lend a definite picturesque and dynamic quality to the composition of the building.

The lavishly adorned gallery attached to the monumental Church of the Resurrection and having a number of arches over the windows and "towels" with coloured tiles under them, provides a contrast to the church. The slender central volume of the church corresponds to the unusual height of the well-lit interior. Instead of a traditional wooden iconostasis, we see here a solid wall covered all over with several tiers of images. The lower tier is converted into an arcade, the columns of which decrease in height towards the sides of the chancel wall. They are supplemented

51. The Kremlin. Church of the Resurrection. Ca 1670.
View from the Church of Our Lady (Hodegetria)

52. The Kremlin. Church of the Resurrection. Interior

53. The Kremlin. Church of the Resurrection.
Fresco: The Last Supper. Ca 1675

54. The Kremlin. Church of the Resurrection. Space under the dome

55. The Kremlin. Church of the Resurrection. The gallery and portal

→
56. The Kremlin. Assembly Square. Cathedral of the Assumption
(16th century) and the belfry (1682–87)

by porticoes in front of the Holy Gates and within the chancel behind them. As a result, there arises an illusion that the whole chancel section is a majestic arched colonnade seemingly receding into a distance from the viewer.

The interior of the Church of Our Saviour-at-the-Court has even a more original architectural solution. The solium, or a platform in front of the chancel, is merely encircled in the Church of the Resurrection with a stone balustrade, with icons painted in its recessed "towels". The Church of Our Saviour has a higher and much larger solium, so parishioners are short of room there. This is due, on the one hand, to the fact that this church was intended only for the Metropolitan himself and his close associates, i.e. it served as a domestic church; on the other, Jonah's predilection for ceremonial services attended by dozens of priests and large choirs of singers. But the solium in the Church of Our Saviour is remarkable not only for its dimensions. Its builders achieved amazingly vivid plastic effects. The balustrade of the solium is crowned by an arcade of elaborate double arches with decorative bosses – round melon-shaped finials seemingly suspended from above instead of "missing" columns. The gilt arcade of semi-columns on the chancel wall echoes the similarly decorated columns. The entrances to the chancel are framed with perspective portals, gilt and adorned with painted decoration. The walls over the colonnade bear the painted two-tiered image of *The Deesis*.

The murals in the Church of Our Saviour-at-the-Court executed by the best masters of that period under the guidance of Gury Nikitin, similarly to other churches of Metropolitan Jonah's age, strike us by the mastery of its painters. The frescoes cover the surfaces of the walls and vaults from top to bottom, which demands a high decorative quality of painting. The painters succeeded in finding such intense colour combinations, which, not breaking the unity of the inner space, lent an ornate quality and a festive emotional air to all the interiors. One's attention is attracted by the active use of saturated blue and red tones. Besides the difficult task of attaining a harmonious juxtaposition of such strong contrasts, one should bear in mind that in the seventeenth century these pigments – cinnabar and sky blue colour – were exceedingly rare and expensive. The overall, "carpet-like" arrangement of dozens of various subjects was a tremendously difficult compositional task. The authors of the Rostov murals revealed a rare skill in arranging the rhythm of the linear design uniting all the representations into a single monumental composition. Although the frescoes in the Church of Our Saviour preserve the conventional character of imagery typical of medieval art, immediate life impressions can also be clearly sensed in them. They are evident in the observation of individual everyday details as well as in the treatment of the facial mimicry and the plasticity of bodies used to convey the many-sided psychological images of human characters.

The perfection of three-dimensional and colouristic solutions of the Rostov architectural complex invariably attracted the attention of Russian artists. Among them were Viacheslav Zabelin, a talented painter active in the second half of the nineteenth century, the world-famous artist and scholar Nicholas Roerich and many others. You can always come across a group of students of art schools and colleges painting views of the Kremlin or copying frescoes in the interiors.

Markedly different from other structures in the Kremlin is its latest building – the Church of Our Lady (Hodegetria). Constructed at the very end of the century, it acquired the distinctive features of the "Moscow Baroque" with its elaborate decorative details in relief enlivening the wall and the polychrome treatment of the façades in imitation of a chessboard creating an illusion of faceted planes.

The two monasteries flanking the town – the Monastery of St James in the south-west and the Monastery of St Avraamy

57. The covered gallery around the Kremlin wall

58. The Kremlin. Church of Our Saviour-at-the-Court. 1675. Solium

59. The Kremlin. Church of Our Lady (Hodegetria). 1692–93

THE GOLDEN RING

in the north-east – enhance the vivid impression produced by Rostov. They have common features in their design with the Metropolitan's Court – the Kremlin, as, for instance, the gateway churches with towers on either side. This motif was borrowed from the Monastery of SS Boris and Gleb located on the road to Uglich.

The structures of the eighteenth and nineteenth centuries betray features of the styles which emerged in Russia after the

60. Monastery of SS Boris and Gleb. Founded in the 14th century. The gateway Church of the Presentation in the Temple (1680), the north-western corner tower, the Annunciation Church (1524–26) and the cathedral of SS Boris and Gleb (1522–24, architect Grigory Borisov)

61. Monastery of St Avraamy. Founded in the late 11th – early 12th century. Gateway Church of St Nicholas. 1691, 1826–37

62. The bells are ringing

reforms of Peter the Great such as the Baroque of the European type, Classicism, pseudo-Gothic and Empire. This circumstance, however, did not break the town's spatial unity. The architects who participated in the construction of Rostov the Great, had a rare feeling of the ensemble, which enabled them to integrate the buildings differing both in character and scale with the already formed architectural complexes. As a result the town acquired some new features enriching its skyline.

63. Monastery of St James (founded in the late 14th century). Octagonal tower of the fence. 1780s–1790s

64. Lake Nero. View of the St James Monastery of Our Saviour

65. Monastery of St James. Church of St Demetrius (1794–1802), the Church of the Conception (1686) and the Church of St James (1836)

For many centuries Rostov was famous for its Marketplace and its name was added to that of a nearby church – the Church of Our Saviour-on-the-Marketplace. The Trading Rows designed in the style of Classicism adorned the Marketplace in the nineteenth century. Behind the long building of the rows there soar ancient buildings, including the sixteenth-century Cathedral of the Assumption, another replica of its counterpart in Vladimir. The town was always famous for its master craftsmen: founders, who equipped the belfries of the towns and monasteries with sonorous bells, kitchen-gardeners supplying even St Petersburg with their agricultural products, jewellers and needlewomen specializing in gold embroidery. Of particular renown was the handicraft that developed in the eighteenth century – the art of making filigree articles adorned with a fine enamel pattern over metal. Stalls with these vividly coloured objects became an original and indispensable part of the urban scene.

66. The Trading Rows (19th century),
the Church of Our Saviour-on-the-Marketplace (late 17th century)
and the Cathedral of the Assumption (16th century)

67–71. Souvenir stalls at the Trading Rows

THE GOLDEN RING

UGLICH

Uglich is located not far from Rostov. The first mention of the town in the chronicle dates from 1148. It is situated at the place where the Volga bed makes an abrupt turn, which probably gave its name to the town – from *ugol* ("angle"). According to a different version, the town derived its name from charcoal-burning, which was a popular craft here ("coal" meaning *ugol'* in Russian). There is a legend that even in the pre-Christian times the detachments of the Kievan princes used to come here to collect tribute. Uglich flourished in the fifteenth century when it minted its own coin and construction grew more active. At the end of the sixteenth century, when the Time of Troubles began, Uglich witnessed the tragic events, which largely determined the town's further destiny and left a dark imprint on entire Russian history. On 15 May 1591 Tsarevich Dmitry or Demetrius, son of Ivan the Terrible, the only heir to the crown, died in Uglich. Historians do not agree about the true reason of his death to this day. In any case, popular rumours accused Boris Godunov of being guilty in his death. Godunov, who soon became the Tsar of Russia, failed to win the true recognition of his power from the population. During a mutiny at Uglich Boris's envoys were murdered, and the townspeople, who cherished to see the Tsarevich growing up next to them on the throne, refused to agree with the official explanation of the boy's

←

72. *The Kremlin. Church of St Demetrius-on-the-Blood. 1692*

73. *The Kremlin. Church of St Demetrius-on-the-Blood. Fresco on the western wall showing the murder of Tsarevich Dmitry. 1772*

74. *Icon:* Tsarevich Dmitry

75. *The Kremlin. Church of St Demetrius-on-the-Blood. Iconostasis. 1867*

death as an accident. The troops sent from Moscow meted out punishment to the mutinous population. Several years later the Polish-Lithuanian invaders met a fierce resistance at Uglich. The Uglich people would not accept the version declared by the Poles. The invaders wanted to put on the Russian throne the Pretender, who claimed to be Tsarevich Dmitry allegedly saved from killers sent by Boris Godunov. The town was ravaged and burnt down. Uglich shared the sad destiny of many Russian cities and towns.

76. The Kremlin. Church of St Demetrius-on-the-Blood. Refectory. Frescoes: The Creation of Adam and Eve *and* The Fall. *Painted by Piotr Khlebnikov. 1788*

77. The Kremlin. Church of St Demetrius-on-the-Blood. Passage from the Refectory to the main hall of the church

78. Church of St Demetrius-on-the-Blood. The "exiled" bell. The bell had its loop cut off, the tongue torn out, and after being whipped it was exiled to Siberia. The bell returned to Uglich only 300 years later.

THE GOLDEN RING

At the spot where the Tsarevich had died a chapel was soon put up to be replaced over the years with the Church of St Demetrius-on-the-Blood, at first built in wood and later in stone. Bright colours and sumptuous relief decoration make this church the focal point of a panoramic sight from the Volga.

Of great interest is the destiny of the bell that warned the inhabitants of Uglich about the death of Dmitry. Trying to solve in some way the situation after the Tsarevich's murder, the authorities blamed the bell for arousing disorders.

The popular consciousness, however, has never lost its life-asserting quality. The radiant decor of the Church of St Demetrius-on-the-Blood convincingly proves that as do the majestic look of the Cathedral of the Transfiguration and the festive appearance of the Church of the Assumption in the Monastery of St Alexis (1628), one of the first buildings constructed after the terrible Time of Troubles. The latter church, which became a memorial to the dead Uglich warriors, was aptly called "Beautiful" for its exclusively slender proportions and expressive decor. The relief details

in the lower part of the structure are more restrained, yet even in this section the architects attained an expressive plastic solution. For example, in the arcature fillet running under the cornices of the apses longer semi-columns alternate with shorter ones, which reminds of an arcade with decorative bosses. The relief of the upper tier, crowned with three tent-shaped tops thrusting upwards, is much more energetic.

Worthy of particular interest is one of the oldest surviving buildings in the town – the so-called Chambers of Tsarevich

79. The Kremlin. Church of St Demetrius-on-the-Blood
and the Cathedral of the Transfiguration (1713)

80. Monastery of St Alexius. Founded in 1371.
Church of the Assumption (the "Magnificent Church"). 1628

81. The Kremlin. Chambers of Tsarevich Dmitry. 1482

82. The Kremlin. Cathedral of the Transfiguration. Iconostasis. 1860

Dmitry, if somewhat distorted by an unskilled repair in the nineteenth century, but still retaining a part of specific decorative elements (ornamental bands, triangles, etc.), which allow us to presume that masters from Pskov or Novgorod were active here.

Uglich has been always famous for diverse high-quality products. Thus, the watch *Chaika* produced at the local factory is a generally known trademark nowadays; local cheeses are also popular. In the late nineteenth century the town began to assemble its own museum collections of art objects and the first display of antiquities was opened. In the recent period a new and quite unusual museum has been established in Uglich – the Museum of Vodka. This traditional Russian drink, known all over the world, is represented here in a great variety of brands connected with certain technological secrets. Some part of the display describes the "infrastructure of consumption" – customs associated with the use of strong drinks, their packing and advertising.

83–85. Museum of Vodka

YAROSLAVL

Yaroslavl is the largest and most urbanized city of the "Golden Ring". It was founded at the spot where the Kotorosl River empties its waters into the Volga – the place which seems to be destined by nature itself for the control of this important trade route. A legend associates its emergence with Yaroslav the Wise – one of the most outstanding rulers of Ancient Russia. This event is said to have taken place in the early eleventh century. Yaroslav came to the bank of the Volga with his warriors and performed there the act that signified, in the eyes of the local pagans, the affirmation of a new invincible force – he killed by his battle-axe the totemic She-Bear, the mother of the human race. It is perhaps due to this fact that the loyalty of the inhabitants of Yaroslavl, even during the age of the most ferocious feuds and troubles, to the power of the grand dukes. And the She-Bear holding an axe appeared on the scarlet field of the coat-of-arms of the Yaroslavl Principality. The city could recover after trials and tribulations. It suffered the greatest damage from the onslaught of the Mongol-Tartar hordes, and a terrible fire in the middle of the seventeenth century turned Yaroslavl into a desert covered with ashes. The energetic construction in the city after fires when every customer – usually a settlement or a rich merchant ("guest") sought to challenge his rivals in the perfection of the building under construction and as a result evolved a highly representative, "Yaroslavl" type of church. While being close to the general Russian five-domed church with a tent-shaped bell-tower, the local variety is marked by an exclusive expressiveness of its proportions, original constructive and decorative solutions, inimitable colour range of glazed tiles on its façades and poetic frescoes in its interiors.

The Church of St John the Baptist at Tolchkovo appeared as a kind of structure typifying Yaroslavl architecture of the seventeenth century. The traditional tent-shaped design was replaced here for the bunches of five-domed groups. This novel design developed an architectural motif of the five central domes creating the unique composition of fifteen domes over a single roof. The exceptionally rich decoration of the façade of the Church of St John the Baptist matches the original solution of the openwork many-tiered bell-tower.

←
86. The Korovniki Settlement. Church of Our Lady of Vladimir (1669) and the Church of St John Chrysostom (1649–54)

87. The Kotorosl River. View of the Church of St John the Baptist at Tolchkovo

88, 89. Church of St John the Baptist. Details of the façade decor

90. Church of St John the Baptist. The portal and the gallery

91. Church of St John the Baptist. 1671–87

THE GOLDEN RING

The Monastery of Our Saviour was the essential link in the urban ensemble of Yarosavl for many centuries. Various structures built in the course of several centuries were preserved there. The earliest of them dated from the early sixteenth century. These are the Cathedral of the Transfiguration and the Holy Gate with a watch tower. Incorporated into the system of urban fortifications, the monastery played the role of the most important fortification, too. Thus, in the early seventeenth century it successfully withstood the attacks of the Polish-Lithuanian invaders. It is no less important that the monastery was a major cultural centre – the first school in north-western Russia was opened in it and a number of first-rate works, now part of the golden treasury of Russian art, were produced in the monastery. Its extensive library preserved a number of literary rarities including the world-famous epic poem *The Lay of Igor's Host*. This most ancient masterpiece of Russian literature made admit the fact of the existence of a well-developed culture in Russia even in the twelfth century. The monastery has retained its educational role to this day – its territory houses a museum of history and architecture with a very rich collection of icon-painting and decorative and applied art and a special department devoted to *The Lay of Igor's Host*.

The Cathedral of the Transfiguration was designed under the influence of the Moscow Kremlin cathedrals constructed in the late fifteenth and early sixteenth centuries. This influence

92. Monastery of Our Saviour. Founded in the 12th century

93. View the Monastery of Our Saviour from the north-west

94. Monastery of Our Saviour.
The Metropolitan's Chambers. 17th century

95, 96. Trading stalls at the Monastery of Our Saviour

97. Monastery of Our Saviour. Beehives

→
98. Monastery of Our Saviour. Saint Gates' Tower (1516), the belfry (16th century), the Church of the Entry into Jerusalem (1617–19) and of the Yaroslavl Miracle-Workers (1827–31, architect P. Pankov), the Cathedral of the Transfiguration (1506–16)

accounts for the amazing harmony of proportions of the building attained thanks to the use of the single modular measure, 1.75 m, during its construction and clear-cut outlines of details. The austerity of the principal volume is enlivened by a special rhythm of the open two-tiered arcade of the covered gallery at the western façade, which creates, together with the three-domed top receding into the distance, an entertaining play on the ledged volumes.

The frescoes in the Cathedral of the Transfiguration, which date from the sixteenth century, are the earliest ones among the surviving Yaroslavl complexes of murals. They make up a vivid page in the chronicle of Russian monumental painting and foresee its brilliant flourishing in the subsequent century. The Yaroslavl frescoes created in the seventeenth century have survived in many churches and are a unique phenomenon in Russian art. Their abundance, good state of preservation and exceptional artistic merits make a visit to this ancient city especially rewarding.

The colour scheme of the murals in the Cathedral of the Transfiguration is devoid of the loud polychrome quality of the seventeenth-century frescoes – it is based on the exquisite combinations of silvery-pearly, purple-brown, pale pink and greenish tints. The multifigured scenes are marked by a narrative character and an inclusion of a large number of everyday details (attributes, clothes, weapons, etc.). This was caused by an aspiration to make the basic church dogmas accessible and convincing for parishioners of the sixteenth century, a period characterized by an extreme abundance of heretic movements. In the depiction of individual characters painters paid more attention to the expressiveness of silhouettes and the resonance of colour spots. One's attention is immediately caught by the monumentally treated image of St John the Baptist, whose figure is skilfully arranged on the curvilinear surface. Strikingly varied are the so-called "towel" motifs – decorative representations of draperies in the lowest tier of the murals. They are based on variations of a single theme – a circle framed by a combination of squares, lozenges and stars. All these elements have a symbolic meaning and create by their alternating pattern a measured melodic rhythm.

The north-western pillar of the Cathedral of the Transfiguration retains a rare evidence from that period – a hall-mark featuring the names of the artists: "And signed by the Moscow masters Larion Leontyev the Junior, Tretyak and Fiodor Nikitin, as well as the Yaroslavl artists Afanasy and Dementy, Isidor's children." The primary position of the Moscow masters is notable, for during the subsequent century they will cede their priority to local and Kostroma painters.

The bell-tower affords a fine panoramic view combining quite different elements: forests receding into the distance behind the river, medieval structures and the living quarters of the contemporary dynamic city. Yaroslavl happily evaded the fate that befell to the majority of provincial cities and towns, which underwent drastic restructuring during the age of Catherine the Great to conform to the laws of regularity. As a result a number of important ancient architectural landmarks were irreparably lost. This city on

99. Monastery of Our Saviour. Cathedral of the Transfiguration

100. Monastery of Our Saviour.
Cathedral of the Transfiguration. Interior

101. Monastery of Our Saviour. Cathedral of the Transfiguration.
Fresco showing St John the Baptist. 1563–64

102. Monastery of Our Saviour. Cathedral of the Transfiguration.
Fresco: The Last Judgement. 1563–64

THE GOLDEN RING

YAROSLAVL

THE GOLDEN RING

the Volga is an example of a careful attitude to architectural monuments. Ancient buildings became in Yaroslavl both architectural accents and principal structural elements during the creation of its new up-to-date layout. Thus, one of the finest buildings of the Pre-Petrine era – the Church of the Prophet Elijah – turned into the dominant landmark of Yaroslavl and the focus of the new system of radiating streets. This church combines in its present-day appearance calm and clarity with dynamism, while its frescoes show both touching lyricism and decorative monumental quality.

←

103, 104. View from the belfry in the Monastery of Our Saviour

105–107. Church of the Prophet Elijah. 1647–50

The specific feature of Yaroslavl is that it was built up in a steady manner and there were no intervals in its construction from the eighteenth century onwards. The appearance of Yaroslavl is very organic in that the medieval, pre-Petrine buildings do not clash here with the contemporary housing construction based on the developed industry and modern infrastructure. Besides the famous landmarks of ancient Russian architecture, worthy of special interest in Yaroslavl are also mansions and social buildings put up in the eighteenth to twentieth century, which reflect an evolution of styles in the past ages. The building of the local theatre (named after Fiodor Volkov, a creator of the Russian professional theatre born in Yaroslavl) is a tribute to the neo-Classical style of the early twentieth century. The elegant stylization of the Chapel of St Alexander Nevsky in the "Russian style", a work of the late nineteenth century, was designated to emphasize the continuity of the past cultural traditions. An expressive pavilion in the neo-Classical style is erected at the high embankment of the Volga, which affords a magnificent panoramic view of the great Russian river.

108. Chapel of St Alexander Nevsky. 1892. Architect N. Pozdeyev

109. Church of St Nicholas ("at the Timber Town"). 1695

110. View of the Volga

111. The Volga embankment. Railing and pavilion. First half of the 19th century

THE GOLDEN RING

KOSTROMA

A little downstream the Volga from Yaroslavl lies Kostroma, a city the history of which is full of mysteries because ancient chronicles almost do not mention it. Some indirect records enabled Vasily Tatishchev, a noted eighteenth-century historian, to suppose that Prince Yury Dolgoruky founded Kostroma in 1152. Not participating in the struggle for leadership and having no ambitions to become the grand princes' capital, this city won the glory of the "linen capital of the north" – in the Middle Ages it produced the world's best linen. It was not accidental that the coat-of-arms of Kostroma includes a golden ship with its sails filled out by the wind. Kostroma was a major trade centre of Russia and merchants from the greatest maritime state of the world, England, used to come here to purchase goods. The city, which stood at the outward bounds of the then cultivated lands, was not only engaged in trade, but also not infrequently served as a strategic point. It was in Kostroma that the grand princes Dmitry Donskoy in 1382 and his successor Vasily I in 1408 saved themselves during the Tartar-Mongol invasion. In the sixteenth century Kostroma was the point from which regiments set out for campaigns against the Kazan Khanate and in the seventeenth century False Dmitry tried to find shelter here from the Russian popular militia. The city was a temporary seat of Mikhail Fiodorovich, the first Tsar of the Romanov Dynasty. In the winter of 1613, at the price of his own life, the peasant of the Kostroma district Ivan Susanin saved the Tsar from the Polish invaders.

The gem of the city's outskirts is the Ipatyevsky Monastery named after St Hypatius. The monastery spreads in a picturesque way along the bank of the Kostroma River not far from the place where it empties its waters in the Volga. The former monastery now houses the open-air Museum of History and Architecture famous for its rich collections. A variety of architectural motifs and observation points make this complex a unique tourist landmark.

The monastery was founded in the 1330s by the former Tartar *murza* Chet who adopted the Orthodox faith. In the sixteenth

←

112. View of the Ipatyevsky Monastery (founded in the 1330s)
from the Kostroma River. In the foreground, the Church
of St Chrysanthus and St Darya

113. Ipatyevsky Monastery. The "New Town". South-western tower

114. Ipatyevsky Monastery. View of the gateway Church
of St Chrysanthus and St Darya (1862, architect Konstantin Thon)
and the Archbishop's Block (1840–60)

115, 116. Ipatyevsky Monastery. The "New Town".
Round north-western and south-western towers
and the central "Green" Tower. 1642–43

117. Ipatyevsky Monastery. The "Old Town".
Square tower. 1586–90

118. Ipatyevsky Monastery. The "New Town".
Open galleries-passageways around the walls

119. Ipatyevsky Monastery. The "New Town".
Church of the Transfiguration from the village of Spas-Vezhi. 1628

120. Ipatyevsky Monastery. Carved gate

121. Part of the museum display

122. Ipatyevsky Monastery.
Chambers of the Boyar Romanov Family. 16th–19th century

century the monastery turned out to be connected with his descendants – the influential Godunov family. The rich monastery with the family's burial place was to show that political ambitions of its patrons were well grounded.

During the Time of Troubles the monastery buildings and defensive structures suffered a great damage. The present-day appearance of the Ipatyevsky Monastery took shape in the subsequent period. To the Old Town, which had existed as early as the fifteenth century, a plot of land was added in 1619 that was named later the New Town to contrast it with the earlier complex. The territory was marked with three towers, the middle one of which, the many-tiered Green Tower, became the main entrance to the monastery. Worthy of special interest among the early structures is the belfry of the late sixteenth century. The gateway Church of St Chrysanthus and St Darya, built in the Russo-Byzantine style in 1862 according to a project by Konstantin Thon, blended well with the monastery's complex completing it.

The most significant structure of the monastery is the Cathedral of the Holy Trinity constructed by the Godunov family in imitation of the stately examples of Moscow architecture from the mid-seventeenth century. The formidable and expressive shapes of the basic volume of the building are highlighted by

123. Ipatyevsky Monastery. Cathedral of the Holy Trinity. 1650–52

124, 128. Ipatyevsky Monastery. Belfry. 1603–05

125–127. Bells of the Ipatyevsky Monastery belfry

KOSTROMA

the ample decor of the apses. The ornate porch attached to the cathedral also contributes to its compositional variety.

All the walls, pillars and vaults of the cathedral are adorned with frescoes. The ornamental stamp on the southern wall preserves the inscription mentioning nineteen mural painters: "This holy church of the city of Kostroma was decorated by Gury Nikitin, Sila Savin, Vasily Osipov, Vasily Kozmin..." This large team succeeded to embellish the cathedral with murals in 1685 during a single summer. The team included the best masters of that period summoned from different cities and towns – from Yaroslav, Uglich and Rostov. They created joyful, sonorous, well-harmonized complexes of murals including a wealth of decorative, especially plant or "grass" motifs, as they were then called. In the eighteenth century the interior was enriched with a Baroque iconostasis. Its elaborate design perfectly matches the chromatic "polyphony" of the murals and icons.

Kostroma boasts a rich and varied colection of wooden sculpture, the earliest in Russia. One can hardly understand the imagery created by local masonry builders without some knowledge of wooden architecture. Many architectural forms had been evolved and originally realized in wood. For example, the expressive tent-shaped structure of church roofing, known in masonry

129. Ipatyevsky Monastery. Cathedral of the Holy Trinity.
Icon: The Virgin Hodegetria. 17th century

130. Ipatyevsky Monastery. Cathedral of the Holy Trinity.
Icon: St Hypatius of Gangra. 17th century

131. Ipatyevsky Monastery. Cathedral of the Holy Trinity. Interior

132. Ipatyevsky Monastery. Cathedral of the Holy Trinity.
Iconostasis. 1756–58. Carvers Piotr Zolotarev and Makar Bykov

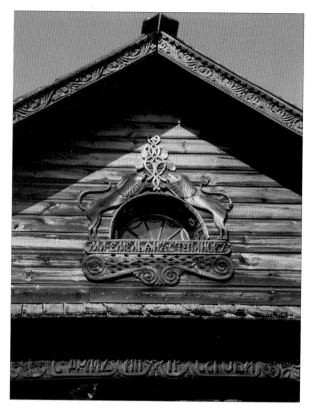

since the sixteenth century, had earlier been employed in wooden church architecture. There are also other examples when devices employed in wooden construction were later used in stone architecture. The emphasis on a decorative quality characteristic of seventeenth-century structures was retained as a typical feature in the decor of interiors in common dwellings until the twentieth century. Representations of mythical creatures and real figures as well as interlacing ornamental patterns played the role of guarding symbols protecting homes from evil spirits. The semantic background had been forgotten over the years and the decorative elements of peasant wooden houses are perceived nowadays just as pieces of artistry. Since many villages were flooded in spring in this area, peasant houses in them were as a rule raised over the ground level. The well-known poet Nikolai Nekrasov described the houses of this type in his poem *Old Man Mazay and Hares* describing a flood in the environs of Kostroma: "Water floods all this locality / So that the village floats up in spring / Like Venice..."

The emergence of Nekrasov's poetic lines devoted to the Kostroma land is not a mere coincidence. The beauty of this countryside never failed to inspire artists and men of letters. The work of the great playwright Alexander Ostrovsky is associated with Kostroma. The elegant pavilion on the bank of the Volga bears his name. The eminent artist Boris Kustodiev visited Kostroma and its environs several times and created here a number of superb and now famous canvases, faithfully capturing the original way of life of merchants in Volga towns. His images are a bit idealized and at the same time tinged with irony.

The Church of the Resurrection-on-the-Debra stands out even among the richly decorated churches of Kostroma. Built simultaneously with the Cathedral of the Holy Trinity and similar

133. Ipatyevsky Monastery. Museum of Wooden Architecture. Log cabin. 1860s. Detail of carving bearing the hallmark of the master craftsman Yemelyan Stepanov (Zirin)

134. At work

135. Ipatyevsky Monastery. Museum of Wooden Architecture. Log cabin. 1860s

136. Ipatyevsky Monastery. Museum of Wooden Architecture. Log baths from the village of Zharki. 19th century

137. Ipatyevsky Monastery. Museum of Wooden Architecture. Church of the Assumption (1721) and an octagonal chapel (19th century) from the village of Fominskoye

to it in design, it is distinguished by a greater wealth and variety of details. The portal of its gate remarkable for its asymmetric design is adorned with relief representations of mythical creatures. A beautiful legend about the construction of the Church of the Resurrection-on-the-Debra has reached us. The merchant Cyril Isakov found a barrel of gold among the goods received from London in exchange for canvas. English businessmen informed their amazed partner that it was to be used for a project pleasing to God. And they say that the merchant donated his money for the construction of this church.

The Gostiny Dvor or Trading Arcade was the heart of the marketplace. The strictly functional building opens up a series of civil structures of the late eighteenth and early nineteenth centuries. These magnificent buildings resolved in the Classicist style shape the centre of Kostroma. A veritable masterpiece of Classicism is the fire alarm-tower tenderly dubbed the "horse-shoe" by the inhabitants of Kostroma. The alarm-tower became a major landmark in the ensemble of the central square and so the main highways of the city, planned in a regular way after a fire of 1773, divert in a fan-like manner from it.

138. *Red or Fine Rows (Trading Arcade). 1789–1800. Architect Karl von Kler*

139. *Fire alarm-tower. 1823–26. Architect P. Fursov*

140. *Church of the Resurrection-on-the-Debra. 1651*

141. *View of the spit of the Volga*

VLADIMIR

Vladimir is one of the most ancient and beautiful cities of Russia. It was founded at the end of the tenth century by Prince Vladimir the Red Sun or, according to another chronicle, by Vladimir Monomachus at the beginning of the twelfth century. In the middle of the twelfth century, under Andrew Bogoliubsky, Vladimir became the centre of North-Eastern Russia and later grew into the main city of the entire Russia. The position of Vladimir, lying on the high hills along the river valley, recalls that of Kiev located on the steep banks of the Dnieper. Moreover, the names of some rivers in the neighbourhood of Vladimir – Lybed, Irpen and Pochaina – were directly borrowed from those in the Kiev region. The new all-Russian capital, a forerunner of Moscow and St Petersburg, originally was called Vladimir-on-the-Kliazma to differ the city from its southern namesake, Vladimir-Volynsky (of Volhynia). The Vladimir princes set themselves the task of building a city rivalling the beautiful Kiev in magnificence.

The period of flowering of Vladimir's white-stone architecture, not long in terms of history, has left us a number of masterpieces of world significance, now on the UNESCO list. The Cathedral of the Assumption was for a long time the principal church of Ancient Russia. This building started the formation of the distinctly Russian architectural school. The perfection of its architectural image led to taking the cathedral in Vladimir as a model for a whole number of major churches in Ancient Russia. Thus, it was to Vladimir that Aristotle Fioravanti, invited from Italy to build cathedrals in Moscow, was sent to study Old Russian architecture on his arrival to Russia. As a result the Italian architect modelled on the Vladimir masterpiece of ecclesiastical architecture Moscow's Cathedral of the Assumption that was in turn the principal cathedral of the Orthodox Church for a long time.

Grand Prince Andrei Bogoliubsky began the construction of Vladimir's Cathedral of the Assumption in 1158. Completed after a devastating fire of 1185 that caused dangerous cracks in the walls, it was redesigned into a five-domed one. As a result the building acquired light and at the same time formidable, monumental proportions. The exquisite carved decor combined with gilding of some elements makes the façades of the cathedral ornate and majestic. The surviving fragments of murals painted by the great Andrei Rublev and his closest assistant Daniel Chorny

←

142. Cathedral of the Assumption. 1158–60, 1185–89

143. Cathedral of the Assumption. Interior

144. Panoramic view of the Cathedral of the Assumption, the bell-tower (19th century), the administrative building of the Vladimir Province (1785–90) and the Cathedral of St Demetrius (1194–97)

145, 146. Cathedral of the Assumption.
Fresco: The Last Judgement. By Daniel Chorny. 1408. Detail
Fresco: The Last Judgement. By Andrei Rublev. 1408. Detail

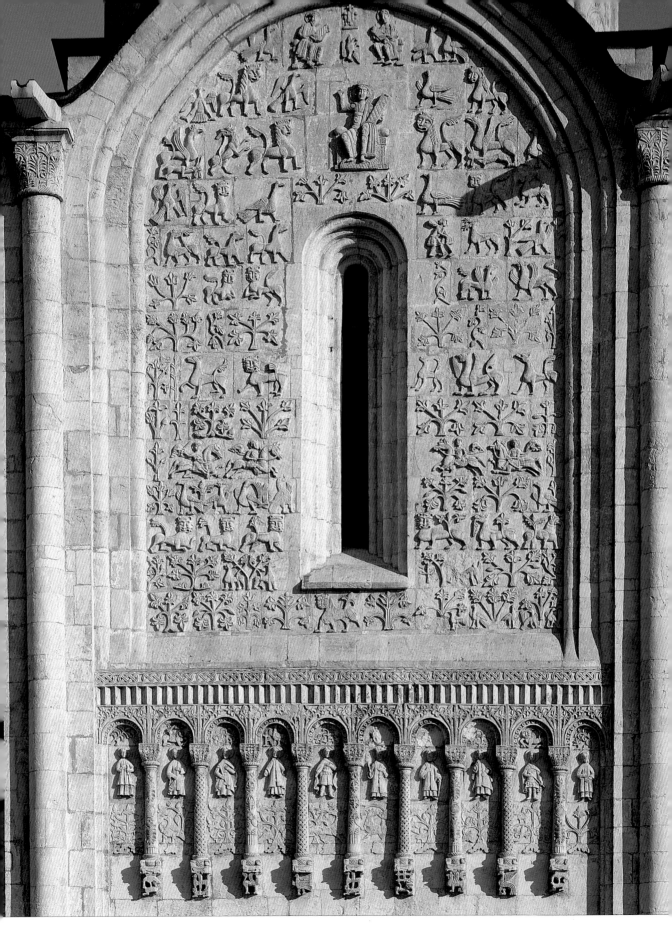

still further enhance the significance of the cathedral. The age known as the Russian Renaissance yielded superb examples of absolutely original artistic solutions such as the fresco *The Last Judgement* in the Cathedral of the Assumption in Vladimir. Devoid of an accustomed mood of catastrophe and vengeance, it evokes a feeling of the ultimate victory of divine harmony.

The most beautiful church of Vladimir, despite the losses inevitable for centuries-long history, is the Cathedral of St Demetrius notable for the rare integrity of its main cubic volume and the elegance of its proportions. But it is not to these qualities that the cathedral owes its outstanding place in world art. Built a little later than the Cathedral of the Assumption, it marked the next phase in the evolution of Russian white-stone architecture distinguished by a strikingly rich outward sculptural decor of churches. The arrangement of the decor in many tiers reflects medieval cosmogonic notions. We easily recognize here biblical characters and Alexander the Great, as well as the donator himself, Prince Vsevold the Large Nest, with his sons. Human figures are combined with plant motifs interpreting the theme of the eternally flowering Tree of Life. Particularly many-sided is the meaning underlying the representations of animals, which are treated with an amazing variety and imagination. These images include horses carrying riders and personifying a victory over evil forces; absolutely fantastic

147. Cathedral of St Demetrius. Detail of the façade

148. The Princess (Kniaginin) Convent of the Assumption (founded in 1200), Cathedral of the Assumption (15th–16th century)

149. Cathedral of St Demetrius. 1194–97

creatures whose appearance reflects the infinitely complex character of the world; scenes of tearing which can be interpreted as a struggle of opposite tendencies in life. The reliefs of the Cathedral of St Demetrius, creating a very vivid play of light and shade, seem to dematerialize the mass of the masonry and lend to the cathedral an impression of lightness in contrast to the monumental bases of the semi-columns shaped like beast paws.

150. Church of St Nicetas. 1762–65

151. Panoramic view of Vladimir

152. Church of the Holy Trinity (1913–16, architect S. Zharov) and the Golden Gate (1164)

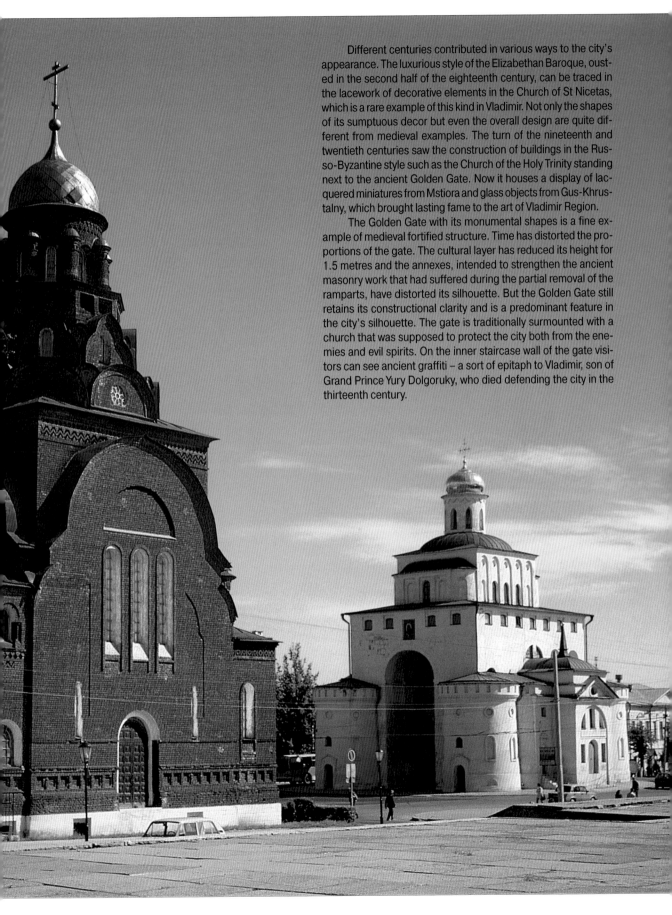

Different centuries contributed in various ways to the city's appearance. The luxurious style of the Elizabethan Baroque, ousted in the second half of the eighteenth century, can be traced in the lacework of decorative elements in the Church of St Nicetas, which is a rare example of this kind in Vladimir. Not only the shapes of its sumptuous decor but even the overall design are quite different from medieval examples. The turn of the nineteenth and twentieth centuries saw the construction of buildings in the Russo-Byzantine style such as the Church of the Holy Trinity standing next to the ancient Golden Gate. Now it houses a display of lacquered miniatures from Mstiora and glass objects from Gus-Khrustalny, which brought lasting fame to the art of Vladimir Region.

The Golden Gate with its monumental shapes is a fine example of medieval fortified structure. Time has distorted the proportions of the gate. The cultural layer has reduced its height for 1.5 metres and the annexes, intended to strengthen the ancient masonry work that had suffered during the partial removal of the ramparts, have distorted its silhouette. But the Golden Gate still retains its constructional clarity and is a predominant feature in the city's silhouette. The gate is traditionally surmounted with a church that was supposed to protect the city both from the enemies and evil spirits. On the inner staircase wall of the gate visitors can see ancient graffiti – a sort of epitaph to Vladimir, son of Grand Prince Yury Dolgoruky, who died defending the city in the thirteenth century.

BOGOLIUBOVO

Bogoliubovo occupies a special place among other highlights of the "Golden Ring". This is the only surviving complex, even if with inevitable losses and alterations, that may be called a medieval castle. Prince Andrei Bogoliubsky preferred to build a reliable residence for himself not in Vladimir, but several miles away from the city, because he sensed a danger coming from his boyar entourage. The area chosen for the construction was exceptionally beautiful and perfectly suited for such architectural projects. The castle-monastery stands on a hill at the edge of a river valley and the solitary Church of the Intercession can be seen nearby, on the low land, amidst water-meadows. Legend has it that the choice of the residence was foreordained in the heavens. During Prince Andrei's travel from the south to Rostov his horses carrying the miraculous icon the Mother of God stopped at the site where Bogoliubovo would be built. During the night the Virgin Mary appeared to the prince and promised Her heavenly patronage to him. The church was put up in honour of the new feast, the Inter-

cession of the Virgin, established by the Prince of Vladimir and the city's priesthood without a sanction of the Metropolitan of Kiev. This feast symbolizing the protection of the Mother of God, was destined to become one of the most revered in Russia that was thought to be the earthly home of the Virgin. And it befell to the Church of the Intercession on the Nerl River to become a sort of symbol of ancient Russian art – its elegant, easily recognized silhouette embodies the highest accomplishments of Russian medieval culture. Although the church has underwent alterations over the years (the gallery and the white-stone facing of the hill disappeared and the shape of the dome changed), it has not lost its beauty and its lovely appearance sticks in one's memory forever.

The Church of the Intercession on the Nerl became the first memorial ecclesiastical structure in Russia. It was dedicated to the successful campaign against the Volga Bulgars and commemorated the prince's son, Izyaslav, who heroically fought with the enemy and died of mortal wounds in 1164.

The Castle of Prince Andrei Bogoliubsky was rebuilt several times. Only the data of archaeological research and the few structures that have remained of the original buildings allow us to form a notion of the earlier design. Thus, the walls with towers erected in the nineteenth century approximately repeat the outline of the former castle. The silhouette of the entire ensemble, however, was markedly altered by the monumental gateway Church of the Assumption with a bell-tower (1841) and the Cathedral of the Bogoliubovo Icon of the Mother of God (1866). The miraculous twelfth-century icon and the remarkable figure of Prince Andrei himself attract pilgrims to this place. The most revered spot in the monastery is the Staircase Tower. It was here, on the observation platform, by the window affording a fine view of the Nerl, that the first Grand Prince of Vladimir was killed. This stone civil structure, unique for the early period of Russian art, arouses a considerable interest of historians of architecture, too. Its ancient lower part has an openwork arcade of semi-columns resting on the recesses in the wall or on small carved consoles, which was characteristic of Vladimir white-stone architecture.

←

153. Church of the Intercession on the Nerl. 1165

154. Complex of the Bogoliubovo Monastery buildings. Founded in the 12th century

155. The Palace of Prince Andrei Bogoliubsky. The Bogoliubovo Castle. Staircase Tower and passage (12th and 17th centuries) and the Cathedral of the Nativity (12th century – 1751)

156. Church of the Intercession on the Nerl

The Church of the Intercession is close to the white-stone cathedrals of Vladimir. But in this case the specific features distinguishing the Vladimir-Suzdal School from the Romanesque architecture of Western Europe, with which it is often compared, are especially prominent. This church is strikingly light and compact; its proportions evoke a sense of a harmonious melody, and its image as a whole has a joyful, lucid quality about it. It is not a mere coincidence that the main character of the reliefs on the church is the Prophet David, the Psalm Singer – this suggests that the creators of the church were aware of the "musical" character of their work. One cannot fail to notice the truly virtuoso craftsmanship of the carvers who brilliantly coped even with the relief rendering of complicated spatial postures of some figures. The church stands on a high hill and during the spring flood it is protected from the high water. The unusual environment creates an additional artistic effect: the Church of the Intercession soaring upwards over the flooded area seems to be drifting smoothly with the flow of the waters.

157. In the environs of Bogoliubovo

158. A bird's eye-view of the Church of the Intercession on the Nerl

159. Bogoliubovo in the evening

SUZDAL

When a traveller approaches Suzdal, he or she does not need to read the names of localities along the road – it is impossible to confuse this town with no other contemporary or even old Russian town. Suzdal does not meet you by a chaos of precincts and industrial zones, but unfolds in a beautiful panorama punctuated by the striking verticals of churches and bell-towers. It seems that a heavenly fairy-tale city descended to the fertile plain woven with a network of small rivers. The surrounding lands well suited for human habitation were settled even in the pre-Christian times. Archaeological research yielded finds going back to the eighth and ninth centuries A.D. The first mention of Suzdal in the chronicles dates from 1024. Playing a significant role in the life of Ancient Russia, Suzdal frequently found itself in a turbulent whirlpool of dramatic events. It was sacked several times, but each time revived within a strikingly short period. Moreover, the artistic quality of the newly constructed buildings never turned out to be inferior to those destroyed. It is not accidental that UNESCO put Suzdal on the list of the world's most valuable historical places worthy of particular care and it deservedly received the status of museum of a city.

Suzdal was the seat of Grand Prince Vladimir Monomach and his son Yury Dolgoruky. In the middle of the twelfth century, the latter founded near the city, in the village of Kideksha on the bank of the Nerl, his own residence which included a palace and the Church of SS Boris and Gleb that has reached us. It is characteristic of Suzdal in general to invent new forms – this church was destined to become the prototype of white-stone cathedrals to be built in Vladimir. The Church of SS Boris and Gleb appears to be more austere and massive than its Vladimir counterparts, but a number of constructive and decorative devices inherent to the Vladimir school of architecture were used for the first time at Suzdal.

←
160. *Convent of St Alexander. Founded in 1240*

161. *Architectural complex from the village of Kideksha. 17th and 18th centuries*

162. *Sledge riding*

163. *Church of the Transfiguration from the village of Kozliatyevo. 1756*

164. *View of the Convent of St Alexander from the Convent of the Intercession*

165. *The Church of Our Lady of Smolensk (1696–1706), the bell-tower (late 18th century), the Moskvina Mansion (late 17th – early 18th century)*

166. View of the Kremlin

167. Russian tea

The original design of the tent-shaped roofing over the belfry lending an expressive and memorable character to the entire structure was a distinctive feature of Suzdal. Such variety having a smoothly curving outline became commonly known as a "trumpet" for its similarity to the simple folk musical instrument. A desire to make simple things attractive, the assertion of the principles of people's aesthetics, pragmatic and at the same time inspired mentality led to the creation of small architectural ensembles including a bell-tower and two churches all around the town. The other kind, just a tiny one, was in fact a "stone *izba*" repeating the compact, simple forms of a wooden church based on a log cell. The smaller type of church was intended for winter services, for it was easier to warm up this church from a stove in cold time, whereas the larger kind of church was more prominent in the town's silhouette.

Suzdal remained a small town and this fact makes even more striking the abundance of architectural masterpieces on its streets. The range and intensity of construction work in the town was amazing. For example, in the sixteenth century, only in the Kremlin there were erected, besides the stone cathedral, fifteen towers and seven wooden churches! From the fourteenth century onwards the town became the seat of a bishop and at the end of the sixteenth century there was the bishopric at the territory of the Kremlin. This determined the town's role as a major centre of Russian culture and education. Its role grew especially important after Kiev had been conquered by Lithuania. Numerous emerging monasteries and settlements growing around the fortified centre of the town rivalled the bishop's court. Each of them hurried to establish itself by building a church. Not a single Russian town or city could rival Suzdal in the number of churches.

THE GOLDEN RING

Nevertheless, a certain duality characteristic of Russian ecclesiastical history should be mentioned. The formation of Christian centres on the sites of former active pagan cults, as it was in Rostov the Great or later on Valaam Island, as well as a penetration of pagan rites into the ritual system of the Orthodox Church are well-known facts. As for Suzdal, even in the seventeenth century there was a custom to celebrate a wedding at night in a church with abundant refreshments, singing and dancing, with priests sharing the merry-making.

The dominant feature of the town was naturally the Kremlin, a fine view of which unfolded behind the ramparts from the valley of the Kamenka River. Its most important edifice is the Cathedral of the Nativity of the Virgin, the earliest among surviving buildings. It had been put up shortly before the onslaught of Batu Khan's horde on the site of the most ancient settlement in this area. The cathedral became one of the latest structures in the chain of white-stone churches erected in the Vladimir region in the twelfth and thirteenth centuries. Time has altered its appearance. The top was built on in brick and the number of domes was enlarged – originally there were three of them in keeping with the Suzdal tradition. The shape of the domes has also changed. But what has remained unaltered in the cathedral is its monumental quality contrasting with the buildings around it. The very type of church characteristic of the Vladimir region has also been retained – with its façade embellished by carved decor and with its articulation by the verticals of the projecting pilaster-strips and by the horizontal of the arcature band. All these elements, however, play but a minor or even decorative role in the Cathedral of the Nativity of the Virgin.

168. The Kremlin. Cathedral of the Nativity of the Virgin.
1222–25, 16th century

169. The Kremlin. Church of St Nicholas from the village of Glotovo. 1766

170. The Kremlin. The bell-tower of the cathedral. 1635

In 1233, the floors in the Kremlin's Cathedral of the Nativity of the Virgin were covered with majolica slabs of yellow, green and dark brown colours characteristic of this material. During the same year the partly surviving "grass" motifs of the funerary niches were executed. The unique Golden Gates, up to now decorating the southern and western portals, are in a very good state. The 48 separate scenes executed in a complicated technique of "fire gilding" over nielloed copper, feature various episodes from the Holy Scriptures. A strikingly subtle psychological treatment of images in combination with the perfection of form and philosophically profound insight into the subjects depicted suggests the unbroken continuity of the then young Russian culture through the centuries and its connection with the great legacy of Ancient Greece. Highly expressive are lion masks with rings in their muzzles, which served as gate door-knockers.

The Archbishop's Chambers in the Kremlin make up a whole complex of structures dating from the fifteenth to eighteenth century. Of particular interest among them is the pillarless hall of the cross-shaped hall – the main festive interior recalling the Patriarch's Chambers in the Moscow Kremlin. The monumentality of the Archbishop's Chambers contrasts with the slender and dynamic wooden Church of St Nicholas brought to the Kremlin from the village of Glotovo, an example that has laid the beginning of the museum of wooden architecture in Suzdal.

The Convent of the Intercession is a very integral and harmonious architectural ensemble. No original fourteenth-century structures have survived and the earliest buildings in the convent

171. View of the refectory Church of the Assumption (1525)
from the bell-tower of the St Euthymius Monastery of Our Saviour

172. The Kremlin. The Archbishop's Chambers. 17th–18th century

173. The summer Church of St Lazarus (1667),
the bell-tower and the winter Church of St Antipas (1745)

date from the fifteenth and sixteenth centuries, while the walls with towers and galleries were constructed in the eighteenth. Worthy of special note is the Holy Gate (1518) – an elaborate asymmetric composition topped with a gateway church. The architecture of the Cathedral of the Intercession, the main one in the monastery, suggests the blending of some local Vladimir-Suzdal features and the general Russian traditions. The restrained character of its inner decor can be accounted for by the role the convent and the cathedral played in the previous centuries. The convent was used as a place of exile for the women of noble birth and the cathedral served as their burial vault. A story about the fate of one of these unfortunate ladies, Solomonia Saburova, the wife of Tsar Vasily III, has come down to us. Her husband, eager to marry for the second time, confined her to this convent. Accused of bareness, she bore a son after taking the veil and imitated the baby's death and burial to save him from the Tsar's anger. In 1934 this historical version was confirmed by finding... a doll under a small tombstone.

The Convent of the Deposition of the Robe with a tall belltower in the Classical style occupies a dominant position in the area

174. Convent of the Intercession (founded in 1364).
The bell-tower (17th century),
the Cathedral of the Intercession (16th century)
and the gallery (18th century)

between Red and Trade Squares. The Cathedral of the Deposition of the Robe with its characteristic three-domed top must have been built by Ivan Shigonia-Podzhogin, to atone for his sin of participation in the confinement of the guiltless Sophronia Saburova in the Convent of the Intercession. In the next, seventeenth century, to make the convent complex more ornate, a richly decorated parvis of the cathedral and the Holy Gate crowned with two tent-shaped tops – a masterpiece that determined the further evolution of Suzdal architecture – were built. The designers of these structures were the first known architects active in Suzdal.

175. Convent of the Deposition of the Robe (founded in 1207). Cathedral of the Deposition of the Robe. First half of the 16th century

176. Convent of the Deposition of the Robe. Bell-tower. 1813–19

177. Convent of the Deposition of the Robe. Parvis of the Cathedral of the Deposition of the Robe. 1688. Detail. Architects Ivan Griaznov, Ivan Mamin and Andrei Shmakov

178. Convent of the Deposition of the Robe. The Holy Gates. 1688. Architects Ivan Griaznov, Ivan Mamin and Andrei Shmakov

In the centre of the town one can see the trading rows, which have repeatedly attracted the attention of motion-picture studios as an expressive glimpse of traditional life to be filmed "on location". At some distance from the present-day centre of Suzdal is situated the Spaso-Yevfimiev Monastery (or the St Euthymius Monastery of Our Saviour). It was built at the same time as the Convent of the Intercession on the opposite bank of the Kamenka River. The monastery's bears the name of its first hegumen Euthymius. The territory of the monastery now belongs to the Suzdal State Museum-Preserve – several displays within its area introduce visitors to various cultural aspects of life in the Suzdal district, in particular with superb works of jewellery produced in the past. Walking along the monastery walls one can reach the observation grounds on the high bank of the Kamenka unfolding a picturesque view of Suzdal. It is probably the best place to enjoy the views of its monasteries and convents, cathedrals and churches, which decorate the town for centuries or have been brought from the district's villages to the open-air museum of wooden architecture. A glance from the height of the ancient monastery walls allows one to evaluate the scale of man's work at Suzdal and the measure of harmony between man-made accomplishments and the natural environment.

179, 182, 183. St Euthymius Monastery of Our Saviour (founded in the mid-14th century)

180. Trading rows. 1806–11. Architect A. Verhsinsky

181. On the bank of the Kamenka River

→
184. St Euthymius Monastery of Our Saviour. Cathedral of the Transfiguration (1582–94) and the belfry (16th–17th century)

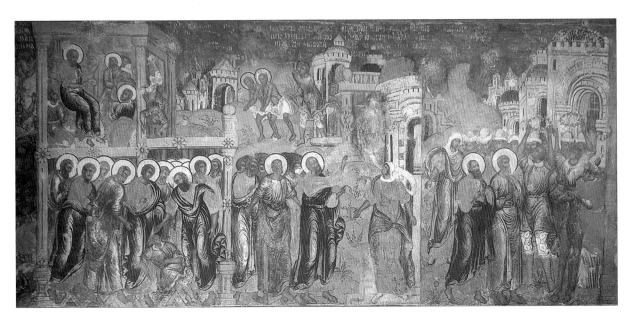

The St Euthymius Monastery of Our Saviour itself houses a collection of remarkable specimens of Suzdal art. Built as a fortified structure, it produces a formidable impression, yet at the same time it is highly poetic and well integrated with the surroundings.

In 1767 the monastery began to be used as a central prison for religious and political dissidents – "insane convicts". They were called so to distinguish them from common criminals not suffering, in the opinion of the authorities, from a derangement of mind. This prison was necessary to Catherine the Great whose policies faced a resistance of various forces.

The main church of the monastery, the Cathedral of the Transfiguration, belongs to the monumental five-domed ecclesiastical buildings widespread in the late sixteenth century. The small slender church (1507–11) over the grave of St Euthymius gives an unusual and picturesque look to the large-scale cathedral. The cathedral itself was not decorated with frescoes for a long time until a team of experienced masters led by Gury Nikitin and Sila Savin began to work on murals in 1689. The frescoes they produced are marked by the combination of strong decorative quality with elaborate complexity drawn from icon-painting intended for viewing at a close range. Such combination was characteristic of the last decades of Russian medieval painting. The "carpet"-like treatment of the overall composition, in which images freely overflow the folds and joints of surfaces, is supplemented here by the use of tastefully designed ornaments. An unusual detail of the murals in the Cathedral of the Transfiguration is the depiction of the Tsars Mikhail Fiodorovich and Alexei Mikhailovich as saints.

Worthy of special attention in the St Euthymius Monastery of Our Saviour is the carefully thought-out concept of its architectural design uniting the buildings that are different in character.

185. St Euthymius Monastery of Our Saviour. Cathedral of the Transfiguration. Interior

186. St Euthymius Monastery of Our Saviour. Cathedral of the Transfiguration. Fresco: The Acts of the Apostles. *1689. Detail*

187. St Euthymius Monastery of Our Saviour. Cathedral of the Transfiguration. Fresco: Christ Carrying the Cross. *1689. Detail*

188. St Euthymius Monastery of Our Saviour. Cathedral of the Transfiguration. Space under the domes

THE GOLDEN RING

Thus, the belfry and the refectory serve as a sort of theatrical coulisses flanking the powerful and majestic edifice of the Cathedral of the Transfiguration. The towers over the railing have different proportions depending on their position: the western and northern ones facing the city and the main thoroughfare, and the southern and eastern ones overlooking the town's outskirts. The architect concentrated primarily on the impression produced by the southern wall owing to its large height caused by the necessity to defend the town from the even plateau. Here the immense Passage Tower was erected. Its dimensions and decoratively designed embrasures made it inaccessible. On passing through the tower the visitor finds himself in a small inner courtyard in front of the gateway Church of the Annunciation. A peculiar accent in the entire ensemble of the St Euthymius Monastery of Our Saviour was the dynamic completion of the refectory Church of the Assumption, which was one of the first in Russia to serve as a model for the development of tent-shaped architecture in the fifteenth to seventeenth century.

The destinies of many well-known historical figures were connected with Suzdal: the Princes Boris and Gleb, the Grand Prince Alexander Nevsky, the Tsar Ivan the Terrible and Prince Dmitry Pozharsky who led the popular militia against the Polish invaders.

Melodic peals of the bells of the St Euthymius Monastery of Our Saviour can be regularly heard over Suzdal. The lower tier of the monastery belfry contains the burial vault of Prince Dmitry Pozharsky. Also preserved there is the mosaic of *Our Saviour* executed in the Imperial Academy of Arts in St Petersburg in the nineteenth century and rescued from a destroyed building.

189. *St Euthymius Monastery of Our Saviour. Gateway tower. 1664*

190. *St Euthymius Monastery of Our Saviour.*
Gateway Church of the Annunciation. Early 16th century

191. *St Euthymius Monastery of Our Saviour.*
The refectory Church of the Assumption. 1525

YURYEV-POLSKOY

Yuryev-Polsky – or, to be more correct, Yuryev-Polskoy – lies on the way from Suzdal to Pereyaslavl-Zalessky. The road passes along the fertile land, which had always attracted the attention of the princes who sought to establish their dominance here. This interest led Yury Dolgoruky to found a town on the yet uninhabited but strategically very important place in the centre of the north-eastern lands, at the spot where the small river Gzy emptied its waters into the then full-flooded Koloksha. Yuryev received an addition "Polskoy" ("standing in the field") to its title so as to distinguish the town both from its southern namesake, like Pereyaslavl and Vladimir, and from the north-western Yuryev standing on the shore of Lake Peipus, the city that has been known as Tartu since 1919. Yury Dolgoruky encircled the fortress with a rampart, which partly survives to this day, seven metres high and about one kilometre long. The most prominent architectural monuments of Yuryev-Polskoy are concentrated within the old town. Of greatest importance among them are the Cathedral of St George, a masterpiece of world significance, and the complex of buildings of the Monastery of the Archangel Michael. Founded in the thirteenth century, the monastery was, however, destroyed several years later by Batu-Khan's horde. The western part of the wall with three towers dated from the middle of the sixteenth century, the earliest among

THE GOLDEN RING

the surviving structures, is strikingly different in its warlike appearance from all the other parts with their small decorative towers.

The main buildings of the monastery were designed in the decorative style of the seventeenth century. Such is the bell-tower surmounted by a tent-shaped top and richly embellished with various elaborate bands. The densely arranged decoration of its lower tiers with carved ornaments resembling ornate towels and decorative niches or "windows" attracts a particular attention. It is remarkable that although the Cathedral of the Archangel Michael was built more than a century later, during the dominance of Classicism in Russia, it was designed in the manner of medieval architecture. The cathedral may be mentioned as one of the first attempts in Russian art of the new times, alongside masterpieces by Vasily Bazhenov and Mikhail Kazakov, at a deliberate stylization to imitate the early Russian tradition. An interesting example of the latter is the Holy Gate surmounted with a gateway church. The gate is an important structure with two archways and two entrances – one for festive occasions and the other for everyday use – are designed with a slight asymmetry lending a vivid air to the monumental structure. Today, the monastery houses a museum that possesses a first-rate collection of ancient wooden sculpture. Notable examples of wooden architecture brought from villages of the

←

192. Monastery of the Archangel Michael. Founded in the 13th century

193. Monastery of the Archangel Michael. The bell-tower (17th century) and the Cathedral of the Archangel Michael (18th century)

194. Monastery of the Archangel Michael.
The wooden Church of St George from the village of Yegorye. 1718

195. Monastery of the Archangel Michael. The Holy Gate (1654) with the gateway Church of St John the Divine (1670)

THE GOLDEN RING

district are also displayed in the open-air museum. But the most important landmark is the Cathedral of St George, the last masterpiece of white-stone architecture built in the Vladimir region.

Constructed later than the churches of Vladimir, Bogoliubovo and Suzdal, the cathedral differs from them by its unusually rich decoration with white-stone carving, which is arranged here, unlike the cathedral's earlier counterparts, in large multifigure and ornamental compositions. One needs a lot of time to see the cathedral's decor owing to its large size and complex character. Unfortunately the cathedral has not reached us in its original state. The building collapsed after a fire and was restored by a team of Moscow craftsmen led by Vasily Yermolin in 1472. He had an experience in restoration, but in this case when many blocks were lost and no measurements had been done in advance, he had a rather vague idea of the cathedral's former image. As a result the appearance of the cathedral we see today has suffered from considerable alterations. Its proportions grew

too heavy and the covering of the main volume rather primitive. Nevertheless the Cathedral of St George produces an overwhelming impression. The eighteenth-century sculptors sought to attain a harmonious unity of figurative and ornamental elements, and the task was easier to fulfil owing to the fact that the decorative features played a significant conceptual role, too. The ornament, executed in a rather low relief, literally covered the entire building serving, with its dynamic pattern and flowing rhythm, as a setting to the more static yet plastically more expressive representations of individual saints and whole narative scenes. The basic motif of the ornament, a winding stem carrying all sorts of trefoils, symbolizes the eternal victory and rejuvenation of life.

196. Cathedral of St George. 1234

197, 198, 200. Cathedral of St George. Details of the façades

199. Cathedral of St George. Southern portal

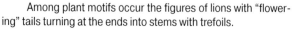

Among plant motifs occur the figures of lions with "flowering" tails turning at the ends into stems with trefoils.

Scholars have established the technological processes used for making such a complicated decorative ensemble. At first one team produced blocks with sculptural images and arranged them in masonry work. Then the linear designs of ornaments were outlined on the walls and the second team of carvers began to work over the completed masonry work. It was the only way to achieve the amazing compositional unity of interwoven ornaments covering large areas. The representations of figures and heads are notable for the use of high relief and even of sculpture in the round, as exemplified by the corner capitals decorated with heads and masks. Among the images depicted occur portraits of historical figures such as Prince Sviatoslav and his warriors. Yuryev failed to become a major trade or industrial centre, but it was always been famous for its skilful craftsmen. No less renowned were the accomplish-

ments of local farmers who successfully cultivated the fertile lands. The fruit of their labours in the form of two baskets filled with cherries decorated the lower field of the town's coat-of-arms.

The Yuryev-Polskoy District is associated with the activities of many prominent people. Thus, the Slavophile Ivan Aksakov was exiled for his views to the estate of Varvarino. Ilya Repin painted here Aksakov's portrait commissioned by Pavel Tretyakov for his gallery. The settlement of Sima, the former estate of the Golitsyn family, is famous as the place where Piotr Bagration, a hero of the war against Napoleon Bonaparte, died from wounds received during the Battle of Borodino.

201, 202. Unhurried pace of life in Yuryev-Polskoy

203. The Church of the Intercession (1769), the bell-tower (second half of the 19th century) and the Church of St Nicetas (1796)

THE GOLDEN RING

THE GOLDEN RING

Texts by *Tatyana Astrakhantseva* and *Victor Kalashnikov*

Translated from the Russian by *Valery Fateyev*

Design and layout by *Denis Lazarev*

Photographs by *Valery Barnev, Sergei Chistobayev, Pavel Demidov, Vladimir Filippov, Alexander Kashnitsky, Victor Savik, Nikolai Rakhmanov* and *Oleg Trubsky*

Edited by *Irina Lvova* and *Irina Kharitonova*

Computer type-setting by *Svetlana Bashun*

Colour correction by *Vladimir Kniazev, Alexander Kondratov, Liubov Kornilova* and *Alexander Miagkov*

ISBN 5-93893-118-5 (Softcover edition)
ISBN 5-93893-138-X (Hardcover edition)

Ivan Fiodorov Art Publishers, 191119, St Petersburg, Zvenigorodskaya ul., 11
Tel./fax: +7(812) 320-92-01, 320-92-11, 320-92-57. E-mail: info@p-2.ru
Ivan Fiodorov Printing Company, St Petersburg (1922)

PRINTED AND BOUND IN RUSSIA